I0759802

HISTORY'S MOST SPECTACULAR HEISTS

HISTORY'S MOST SPECTACULAR HEISTS

HIGH-STAKES THEFTS, INCREDIBLE TREASURES, AND DARING RESCUES

EMMA CARLSON BERNE

weldonowen

Written by Emma Carlson Berne
Designed and edited by Imago Create
Illustrations by Kaja Kajfez/Advocate Art Agency

weldon**owen**

Published by Weldon Owen Children's Books
An imprint of Weldon Owen International, L.P.
A subsidiary of Insight Editions
PO Box 3088
San Rafael, CA 94912
www.insighteditions.com

Weldon Owen Children's Books
Editor: Eliza Kirby
Managing Editor: Mary Beth Garhart

Insight Editions
CEO: Raoul Goff
Senior Production Manager: Greg Steffen

ISBN: 979-8-88674-254-1

Manufactured in China by Insight Editions.
First printing, November 2025. DRM1125
10 9 8 7 6 5 4 3 2 1

Insight Editions, in association with Roots of Peace, will plant two trees for each tree used in the manufacturing of this book.

Contents

Introduction

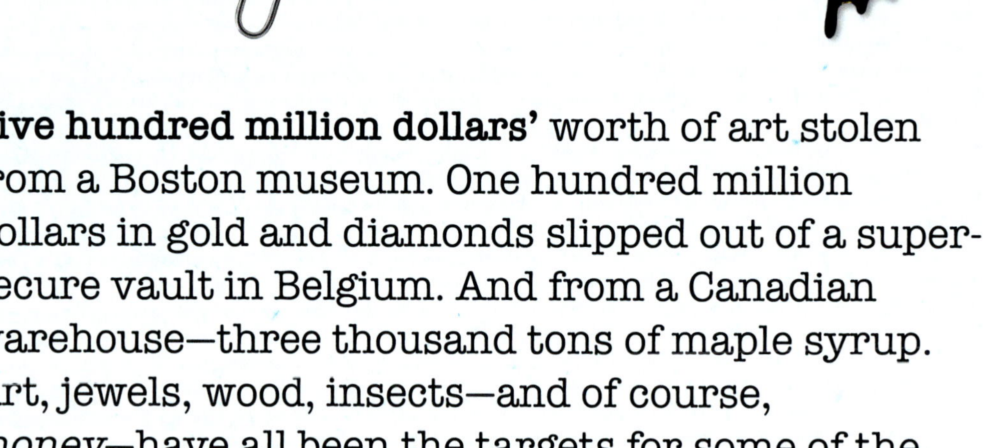

Five hundred million dollars' worth of art stolen from a Boston museum. One hundred million dollars in gold and diamonds slipped out of a super-secure vault in Belgium. And from a Canadian warehouse—three thousand tons of maple syrup. Art, jewels, wood, insects—and of course, *money*—have all been the targets for some of the most devious, clever, and outrageous thefts ever dreamed up by gangs of criminals.

A heist is a robbery, but the crimes explored in this book are more than just simple thefts. Each one was carefully planned and executed *almost* flawlessly. Some have never been solved, despite many clues and hundreds of hours of police work.

Read on to discover details about each captivating caper—thieves disguised as police officers, millions of Japanese yen stolen off the street, one of the most famous works of art in the world hidden in the bottom of a trunk. On each page, test your sleuthing skills and see if you can solve any unsolved crimes. Then flip to the back of the book for a map, timeline, glossary, and other resources to help you investigate the world of smart criminals, dumb criminals, big money, and unsolved crimes.

Buckle up! You're about to dive deep into the dark underbelly of big-time heists.

Who knows just when you might emerge.

Isabella Stewart Gardner Museum Heist

The streets of Boston were dark when a vehicle pulled up outside the Isabella Stewart Gardner Museum on March 18, 1990.

Inside, the museum was silent. The night guard, Rick Abath, sat sleepily at the desk, watching over the priceless artworks in the galleries. He jumped when the door buzzer sounded. Through the intercom, two Boston police officers told the guard that they were here for a disturbance in the building.

No one had reported a disturbance . . . but the men *were* police officers, after all. Rick let them in. And from there, one of the biggest art thefts in the United States began.

Working quickly, the thieves first taped Rick and another guard's mouths shut with duct tape, tied them up, and stowed them in the museum's basement. Then, they went from room to room, slashing paintings from their frames. They snagged drawings and a small eagle ornament. Some of the most famous artworks in the world made it into the thieves' hands, including paintings and drawings by Rembrandt, Johannes Vermeer, and Impressionist masters Edgar Degas and Édouard Manet.

Fast Facts

DATE: March 18, 1990

LOCATION: Isabella Stewart Gardener Museum, Boston, Massachusetts

LOOT: 13 works of art (five paintings, five drawings, an etching, an eagle ornament, and an ancient Chinese brass vessel)

CASE OPEN!

The wealthy philanthropist Isabella Stewart Gardner was also an art collector. In 1903, **she built the museum** to preserve and display her collection. Isabella wrote in her will the art arrangements had to stay the same—forever! Nothing could be changed, added, or subtracted.

Palace Courtyard
The interior courtyard at the Isabella Stewart Gardner Museum was built in the style of a luxurious Venetian palace.

In just eighty-one minutes, the thieves were done. At 2:45 a.m., they drove away from the museum with thirteen works of art worth at least half a *billion* dollars. For hours, the guards were trapped in the musty basement, straining against ropes and handcuffs, duct tape over their eyes and mouths. Finally, the police arrived at 8:15 a.m.

And then the search began. For close to thirty-five years, police detectives and the FBI have searched the art world for these treasures. And for thirty-five years, they've found nothing. The museum has offered a reward of $10 million for information—nothing. The FBI has investigated different suspects, including the Boston mafia, who are known art thieves, and even the museum guard Rick Abath, who died in 2024. Was a wealthy art collector somewhere just dying to get their hands on this artwork—enough to pay someone to steal it?

The case remains unsolved. Out there in the world, somewhere, thirteen works of art are still missing. The empty frames still hang on the walls of the museum, waiting until the day they are filled again.

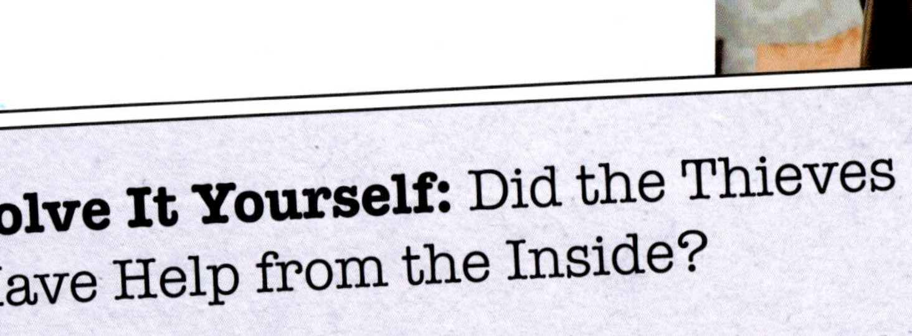

Solve It Yourself: Did the Thieves Have Help from the Inside?

The night guard, **Rick Abath**, opened the museum's side door an hour before the heist. As part of his job, he was supposed to write down what he was doing—but he didn't record this. When the thieves came into the museum, Rick stepped away from the desk, and from the panic button that could call the police. Did Rick really not sense something fishy was going on? Later, police found that motion sensors in part of the museum had been turned off. Did Rick do this to help cover the thieves' tracks?

Empty Frames
The theives cut the paintings out, leaving empty frames hanging on the museum walls.

Edgar Degas painted in the early twentieth century. He was **fascinated by the movements of dancers and horses** and often showed them in his work. His drawing of racehorses and jockeys titled *Leaving the Paddock* was stolen.

The Dutch painter Rembrandt is one of the most famous artists in the Western world. The thieves stole a **tiny self-portrait** he etched. It was only the size of a postage stamp.

Seventeenth-century Dutch artist Vermeer often painted the insides of rooms and houses in exquisite detail. His stolen painting *The Concert* showed a **woman playing a type of piano** while another woman and a man stand and sit nearby.

Hatton Garden Heist

It was going to be one last job. And it was going to be a big one. Six elderly professional criminals, one heavily secured bank vault, and if they could pull this off, enough gold and jewels to set them up for retirement.

Jewel District
The front door of the Hatton Garden Safe Deposit Company is flanked by jewelry shops in London's gemstone district.

Fast Facts

DATE: April 2, 2015

LOCATION: Hatton Garden Safe Deposit Company, London, England

LOOT: £14 million of jewelry, cash, and gemstones

CASE CLOSED!

They picked a perfect target—the Hatton Garden Safe Deposit Company. This bank was located in London's jewelry district. Jewelry makers and dealers had their shops and workshops on the same street. Where would they be stashing their precious gold and gems for safekeeping? The very bank the criminals had their eye on.

For three years, this grandpa-age gang had been planning this heist while at their favorite London pub. Then, over Easter weekend 2015, finally—it was go time.

As soon as the bank employees locked up and left for the weekend, the gang activated. One criminal, an electronics expert known as "Basil," let himself into the Hatton Garden Safe Deposit Company using keys. After disabling the security system, he ran upstairs to let the rest of the gang, dressed as repairmen, into the building using a fire escape.

The thieves were inside. But the safe-deposit boxes they wanted were underground, encased in a concrete vault.

Caper Corner

The ringleader of the group, **Brian Reader**, was also the oldest—he was seventy-seven at the time of the crime. But the Hatton Garden heist wasn't Brian's first caper. He was also part of a gang who robbed a warehouse storing gold and cash in 1983. With the help of one of the security guards, who was in on the crime, Brian and his cronies, masked and armed, burst into the warehouse, beat up the guards, and poured gasoline over them. They threatened to set them on fire if they didn't obey orders to stay down and stay quiet. Then Brian and the gang loaded up **6,800 gold bars** and made their getaway.

With the silence of the empty bank pressing around them, the gang attached ropes and rappelled down an empty elevator shaft. At the bottom lay the vault. Then, it was time for the power tools. Over two days, the criminals smashed through the six-foot-thick concrete wall using crowbars, diamond-tipped drills, and a giant hydraulic ram. They drilled closer and closer, until with a final crash and puff of dust, they were through.

The vault was lined with black safe-deposit boxes from floor to ceiling. The thieves didn't waste time. Forcing open seventy boxes with crowbars, they grabbed jewelry, gold, cash and other treasures worth about £14 million and stuffed the loot into empty wheeled trash cans.

Back outside, the thieves scattered. Some kept loot at home. One buried his in a cemetery. But when an undercover police officer heard one of the thieves bragging about the heist to his buddies in a pub, the game was up. Closed-circuit television footage, license-plate cameras, and cell-phone records soon gave police the names of the six gang members. They were arrested and taken to jail. Later, they were put on trial and sentenced.

But Basil the security system mastermind? He managed to escape capture for more than three years. Finally, he was nabbed also.

Case closed!

Caper Corner

Terry Perkins, another member of the Hatton Garden gang, was a pro as well. In fact, he'd already spent twenty-two years in jail for his part in a 1983 bank robbery. Wearing hoods and carrying shotguns, Terry and the other robbers overpowered the only guard at the **Security Express Bank** early in the morning when the bank was closed. They started loading up cash. As other employees trickled in for work, Terry and the gang took them prisoner, too. They escaped with **£6 million in cash**—the largest bank robbery in England up to that point.

The thieves would have been done breaking into the vault sooner—**if their ram hadn't kept breaking down**. They had to leave to fix it and come back.

Getaway Truck
The gang left the scene in a nondescript white truck.

The gang had another mishap when they finally drilled through to the vault room. **A big metal cabinet on the other side** was blocking their way and was bolted to the floor. Finally, after several tries, they managed to shove it over.

The police gathered evidence on the suspects by looking **at security cameras in the pub** where the criminals gathered after the crime. They used lip-reading techniques to figure out that the gang was discussing how they pulled off the caper.

Empty Boxes
The thieves forced open the doors on the safe-deposit boxes, emptying the contents.

Eugowra Gold Robbery

Frank Gardiner wanted gold—a lot of gold. And he wanted to get it fast. Getting it *legally*? That wasn't a consideration for Frank.

He was an experienced bushranger, an outlaw who lived in Australia's wilderness. Frank ran a cattle-stealing operation out of his butcher shop in Forbes, a brand-new gold rush city in southeast Australia. But he wanted something more than cattle.

Frank and his friends made a plan. The year was 1862, and there was gold to be had in Australia. In fact, miners were digging it out of the ground every day nearby in the British colony of New South Wales. From the porch of his butcher shop, Frank watched gold being loaded into wagons bound for the city of Sydney. The gold wagons were guarded by four men with guns, but there were no guards riding ahead or behind. It wouldn't be hard, Frank told his friends, to help themselves.

Frank and his cronies put their plan into action. On Sunday, June 15, the gang rode out to a spot they'd picked on the road to Sydney, the capital city of the colony of New South Wales. The place was isolated, with a dry creek bed and big boulders—perfect for hiding. The gang blackened their faces to make themselves harder to recognize. Then, they blocked the road with two ox teams and wagons.

Fast Facts

DATE: June 15, 1862

LOCATION: Eugowra, Australia

LOOT: 170 pounds of gold and ten bags of cash, equaling anywhere from $4 million to $10 million in today's US dollars

CASE CLOSED!

Dramatic Recreation
This painting recreates the scene when the gang stopped the wagon and took the gold.

Escort Rock
This large boulder is known as Escort Rock and arks the scene of the gold robbery.

As the gold wagon rattled up the rough dirt road, the gang crouched in the blazing sun, hiding, waiting. The wagon drew closer and closer. Then, the driver of the gold wagon spotted the oxen and wagons blocking the road. He slowed his own oxen. At that moment, the robbers sprang out from their hiding places, guns at the ready. "Hands up!" they shouted, expecting the guards to surrender immediately.

But the guards weren't going to give up so easily. They drew their own guns and fired. The gang fired back. The horses reared in panic, flipping the gold wagon over. Bullets zinged through the air, striking two of the guards. The criminals grabbed two of the horses and loaded them up with the loot from the wagon. Then, they rode off.

When they were far enough away, they opened the bags and boxes containing the gold. They found almost 170 pounds of gold and ten bags of cash. They were rich—and they were wanted.

Eventually, four of the bandits were caught and tried. One gave up information and was pardoned. Frank Gardiner escaped but was later caught by police for other crimes and sent to live in the United States as punishment. And the gold and cash? Police only found a small amount. The rest has never been recovered.

Australia is the only landmass on the planet that is both a country and a continent. Indigenous people have made Australia their home for more than 600,000 years. In 1788, Britian claimed **Australia as a place to send prisoners**. Free British settlers followed and created more colonies. Gold was discovered in 1850, bringing people from all over the world. Australia became an independent country in 1901.

The gang all dressed up in matching **red shirts with red night caps**. It's not clear why—perhaps they thought the matching clothes made them look scarier.

The gang dumped the boxes and the bags containing the loot about **four miles from the scene** of the crime—they took the contents with them!

Caper Corner

The Eugowra robbery was such a success that gang member **Ben Hall** decided to try his luck again shortly after. In March 1865, Hall led a gang out to another remote Australian area and laid in wait for another gold wagon. But this time, when the criminals fired on the gold wagon, the horses got away. Pulling the gold wagon behind them, they fled. A police constable guarding the wagon, **Daniel Byrne**, ran the wagon down, stopped the horses, and ordered the gang to put down the weapons. They fired at him but missed, and eventually, they retreated and escaped. Just two months later, in May, Ben Hall was found by police and shot in a firefight.

Canadian Maple Syrup Heist

It was just supposed to be a routine inspection. The barrels of maple syrup gathered from Canada's vast belts of maple trees were stored in a large government warehouse in Québec, one of Canada's provinces. Eventually, they'd be sold.

Once a year, an official came by to give them a check. In July 2012, inspection day rolled around. The inspector was climbing up on the stacks of barrels and one fell over. That wasn't right. The barrel should be packed full of maple syrup and too heavy to tip. The inspector opened the barrel. It was empty. He started opening more barrels, and more. Others joined in. In the end, they found that almost three thousand tons of maple syrup were gone.

But *gone*? How did three thousand tons of maple syrup just disappear from the barrels? The answer: a group of clever thieves. Over ten months, during 2011 and 2012, these sweet thieves would steal barrels from the warehouse, drive them to a remote cabin, and remove the syrup with hoses. They'd fill the barrels with water to make it harder to tell the syrup was gone. After a while, the game was getting so easy that the thieves didn't even bother to take the barrels off-site. They just started removing the syrup directly in the warehouse and leaving barrels empty and dirty. No one was watching, they figured.

Fast Facts

DATE: 2011–2012

LOCATION: Québec, Canada

LOOT: Almost three thousand tons of maple syrup worth $12.5 million in today's US dollars

And they were right—until the inspector found the empty barrels. Then, the Canadian government realized that a maple syrup theft had been going on right under their noses. There were no security cameras in the warehouse (chalk up one point for the thieves!), so the investigators started examining people who were working in the same industrial park as the syrup warehouse, assuming it would be easy for them break in.

Maple Mayhem
The thieves simply rolled the barrels out of the warehouse without anyone spotting them!

Finally, after months of chasing down leads and questioning suspects, the Québec police arrested the ringleader, Richard Vallières, and more than a dozen others. In the interrogation rooms, they discovered the details of the heist.

Richard Vallières had learned of the syrup barrels from a friend whose wife was the co-owner of the warehouse where the barrels were stored. He knew the syrup was valuable. After removing the syrup from the big barrels, the thieves repackaged it into smaller barrels, then sold it to buyers in Canada and the United States. Some of these buyers might have known they were buying black-market syrup, others thought it was a sweet deal!

In 2016, four years after Canada experienced a serious pancake-topper shortage, Richard Vallières was sentenced to eight years in prison. He also had to fork over (see what we did there?) a fine of $9.4 million Canadian ($6.5 million US).

But North American syrup lovers will be happy to know that the Canadian syrup supply has bounced back. Syrup is now stored in a new, hyper-secure warehouse, complete with twenty-four seven cameras, security walls, and tightly controlled access. Inside, the white barrels are once again stacked high, filled with maple syrup—and safe.

The Canadian government tightly controls the **buying and selling of maple syrup** in Québec. The government even sends out undercover agents to catch people selling syrup from roadside stands.

Sweet Surprise
Every year, Canada exports more than 600 million Canadian dollars of maple syrup around the world.

Caper Corner

Richard Vallières and his cronies aren't the only maple syrup criminals in Québec. In the mid 2010s, maple syrup farmer **Angèle Grenier** would regularly load her syrup into her truck and drive under the cover of darkness to the neighboring province of New Brunswick. There, she'd sell her syrup to a distributor. Why was Angèle ferreting her syrup out of Québec like a criminal? The government of Québec requires farmers like Angèle to sell most of their syrup to them. Then they distribute it. But Angèle and other famers didn't think that was fair. They could make more money selling it themselves! So Angèle did just that. She was caught and went to court. Eventually, she made an agreement with the government and paid a huge fine. If she hadn't, she could have gone to jail.

In the late winter, sap begins to flow in sugar maple trees as the tree prepares for spring. Maple syrup **makers drill small holes into the tree** and let the sap drip out, collecting it in a bucket. This is called "tapping" the tree. The sap is then boiled so that the water evaporates and only the sweet sap is left. It can take about forty gallons of sap to make one gallon of maple syrup!

Tucker Cross Theft

Teddy Tucker was deep under the ocean. It was 1955, and Teddy was looking for treasure—buried treasure. Teddy was diving at the site of the *San Pedro* shipwreck in the warm, turquoise waters off the coast of Bermuda.

Underwater Hunt
Teddy Tucker and his team used underwater breathing tubes to help them explore the wreck of the *San Pedro*.

Fast Facts

DATE: 1975

LOCATION: Bermuda

LOOT: A gold and emerald cross from the fifteenth century

CASE OPEN!

In the fifteenth century, the *San Pedro* sank, and now its rotted timbers lay half-buried in sand at the bottom of the ocean floor. Teddy poked around among the wreckage, and then he saw something flashing in the sand. It was a small, carved gold cross, about the size of his palm, studded with large green gems. Could they be emeralds? Treasure!

Teddy pulled the cross from the sand and carried it back to the surface with him. Experts confirmed that the cross was 22-karat gold and the gems were emeralds. Teddy put the treasure in his closet. He didn't know what he wanted to do with it, but he did know he didn't want to sell it, not yet. He had buyers. One dealer offered him $250,000 in today's money. The American ambassador to Italy offered over $2 million in today's dollars. And eventually, the government of Bermuda claimed the cross was theirs, since it was found in their waters. They wound up buying the cross and other treasures from Teddy and putting them on display at the Bermuda Aquarium.

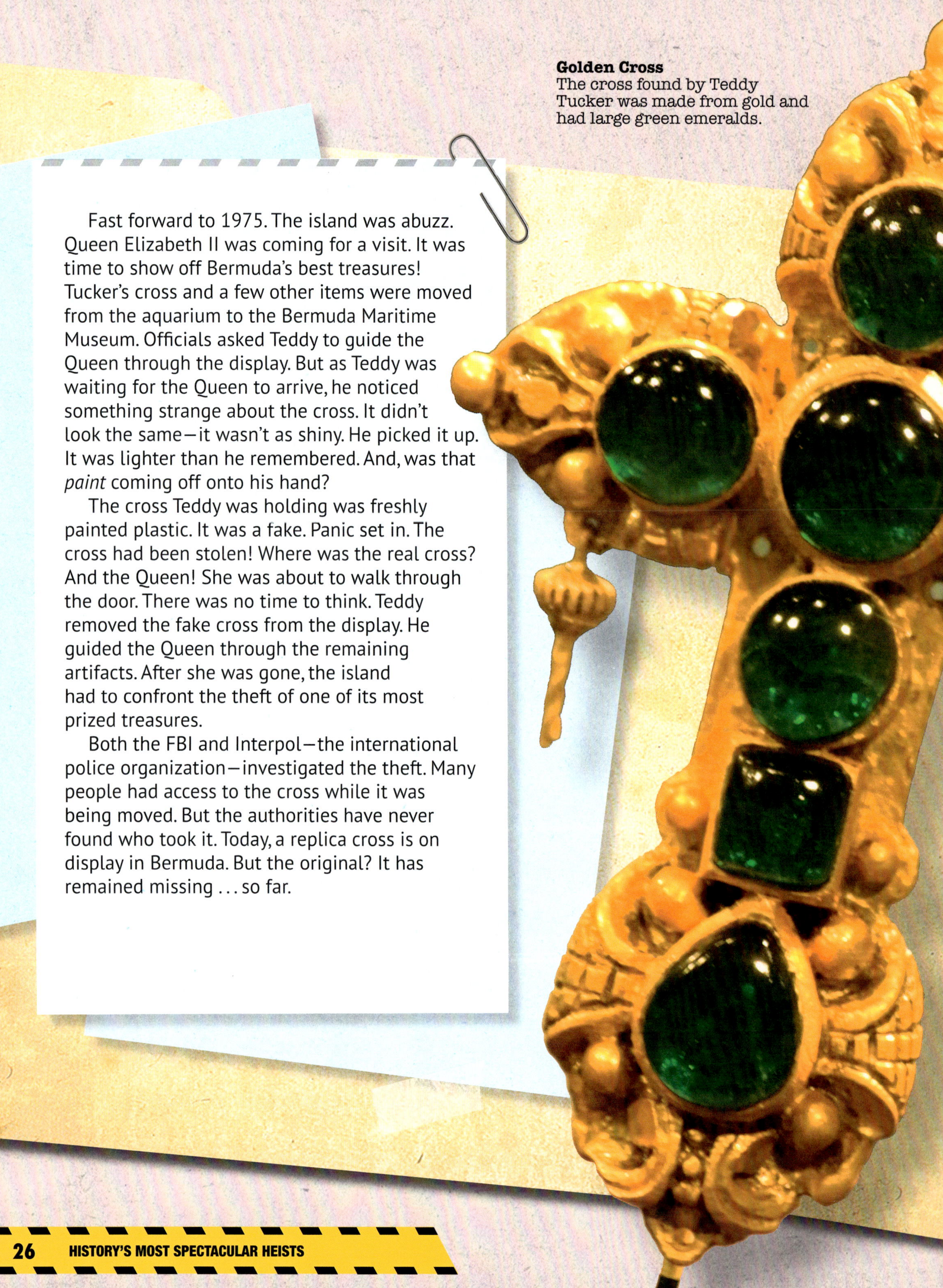

Golden Cross
The cross found by Teddy Tucker was made from gold and had large green emeralds.

Fast forward to 1975. The island was abuzz. Queen Elizabeth II was coming for a visit. It was time to show off Bermuda's best treasures! Tucker's cross and a few other items were moved from the aquarium to the Bermuda Maritime Museum. Officials asked Teddy to guide the Queen through the display. But as Teddy was waiting for the Queen to arrive, he noticed something strange about the cross. It didn't look the same—it wasn't as shiny. He picked it up. It was lighter than he remembered. And, was that *paint* coming off onto his hand?

The cross Teddy was holding was freshly painted plastic. It was a fake. Panic set in. The cross had been stolen! Where was the real cross? And the Queen! She was about to walk through the door. There was no time to think. Teddy removed the fake cross from the display. He guided the Queen through the remaining artifacts. After she was gone, the island had to confront the theft of one of its most prized treasures.

Both the FBI and Interpol—the international police organization—investigated the theft. Many people had access to the cross while it was being moved. But the authorities have never found who took it. Today, a replica cross is on display in Bermuda. But the original? It has remained missing . . . so far.

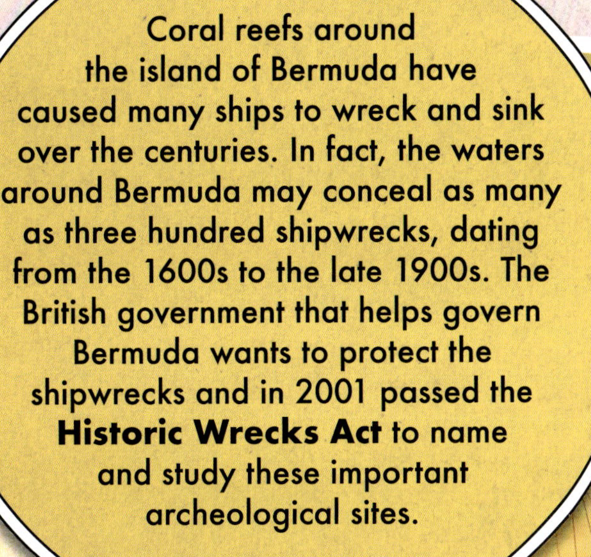

Coral reefs around the island of Bermuda have caused many ships to wreck and sink over the centuries. In fact, the waters around Bermuda may conceal as many as three hundred shipwrecks, dating from the 1600s to the late 1900s. The British government that helps govern Bermuda wants to protect the shipwrecks and in 2001 passed the **Historic Wrecks Act** to name and study these important archeological sites.

Solve It Yourself: Who Took the Cross?

The key to the safe where the cross was stored in the Bermuda Aquarium was kept in an unlocked cabinet, and several different people handled the cross while it was being moved to the Maritime Museum. In fact, because the paint on the fake was still wet, the thief probably switched the crosses sometime during that move. Three different people helped lay out the treasure display, yet no one pointed out the fake. Was one of those people the thief? Teddy Tucker believed that the person who stole the cross had **planned it in advance** as opposed to making a spur-of-the-moment decision. The person had to have had time to make the replica cross, and though many other treasures were on display, only the cross was stolen.

The Last Judgment Heist

The ship *St. Matthew* pitched and bobbed in the ink-colored seas just off the English coast. On board, casks and bundles lay piled on the slimy, damp deck. But under the hold, one particular item was safe, warm, and dry.

It was 1473, and a rich banker named Angelo Tani had commissioned a painting from the German master Hans Memling. Angelo was paying to build a new chapel in a church in Florence, Italy, and he wanted to display this painting on the altar.

Using oil paints on wood, Memling created three panels showing Jesus at the Second Coming—a time when Christians believe that Jesus will return to Earth and judge people's sins. Memling called his painting *The Last Judgment*. Hans had even put Angelo and his wife into the painting. Now the art was wrapped up and headed to Italy on the *St. Matthew*.

But the painting would never reach its destination, because on the night of April 27, pirates from a Polish ship attacked. Slipping over the railings, they took control of the ship and all its loot. They sailed the *St. Matthew* to Gdańsk, Poland. There, the pirate captain divided up the bounty between the crew and the owners of the pirate ship. The Last Judgment wound up on the altar of Saint Mary's, a Polish church.

Three-Part Painting
The Last Judgment by Hans Memling is a tryptich, meaning that it came in three panels that were joined by hinges.

Fast Facts

DATE: 1473

LOCATION: Off the coast of England

LOOT: An oil-on-wood painting

CASE CLOSED!

The painting stayed there until the early nineteenth century, when Gdańsk was under the control of Napoleon and the French. The French thought they might like the painting to go to *their* country, so they took it, much as the Polish pirates had taken it four hundred years before. Napoleon's government was out ten years later, and the painting came back to Saint Mary's.

But *The Last Judgment* wasn't done with its travels. Someone took it out of Gdańsk on the eve of World War II, as museums and churches around Europe were storing and shipping away their treasures in case of bombing. The church was destroyed during the war, but the painting turned up in the State Hermitage Museum in Leningrad (now Saint Petersburg), Russia, where it had been taken as a war prize by Soviet troops. Finally, in 1956, the traveling triptych returned to Gdańsk, where it lives today.

Where in the World

During the many years *The Last Judgment* hung in St. Mary's church, **people lost track of its creator**. They thought that a little scribbled signature meant the painting had been done by the great Dutch master Jan van Eyck. But in 1843, an art historian realized the painting was by Memling, and the artist could receive credit again.

Caper Corner

The pirate **Henry Avery** pulled off a successful heist of his own in 1695 when he and his crew boarded the ship belonging to the world's richest man, the Mughal emperor Aurangzeb. Henry and the gang made off with piles of **gold, silver, sapphires, emeralds, and diamonds**. The loot was worth about $106 million in today's money. But Henry didn't get to enjoy his booty. On the way home from the raid, Henry's ship was wrecked near Cornwall, England, and sank along with its treasure.

At the time of *The Last Judgment* heist, the Polish city of Gdańsk was at war with England. Paweł Beneke, the Polish pirate captain who captured *The Last Judgment*, was **legally allowed to raid English ships** and keep some of the booty. Another one of Paweł's capers? Kidnapping the mayor of London!

Resting Place
Saint Mary's Cathedral in Gdańsk, Poland, where *The Last Judgment* was kept for many years.

Madagascar Rosewood Heist

With a blast piercing the air, the giant ship MV *Oriental Pride* steamed into the port of Jurong, Singapore, and prepared to unload thousands of pounds of cargo from its deck. But the ship was carrying something else.

Not gold, or jewels, or even ivory, but wood—thirty thousand logs of priceless Madagascar rosewood. These logs were just as valuable as art, jewelry, or piles of cash. They could be made into furniture and carvings worth millions. These logs were worth stealing, at least in the eyes of the criminals who conducted the heist.

Rosewood is a rare and precious wood, worth about $1.5 million per cubic meter. Madagascar, an island off the coast of southeast Africa, has more species of rosewood than any other place on Earth. People are not supposed to cut down the trees. They're only supposed to use the wood if a tree falls on its own. But criminals usually don't pay attention to regulations. In the case of the logs aboard the *Oriental Pride*, a Singapore-based company called Kong Hoo paid workers to illegally cut down the trees, then ship the logs across international borders (another crime) and sail them into Jurong Port where they would be unloaded and sold.

Fast Facts

DATE: 2014

LOCATION: Madagascar and Singapore

LOOT: thirty thousand rosewood logs

CASE CLOSED!

Where in the World

Precious Cargo
People load up logs of Madagascar rosewood, ready to ship out to markets across the world.

But now agents from the Singapore government had discovered the heist. The government thought the case would be simple: Kong Hoo would be charged with illegal trafficking, and the logs would be returned to Madagascar.

Lawyers discovered that Kong Hoo had falsified many documents needed for shipping and unloading the logs. But then something strange happened. The government of Madagascar stopped cooperating with the case. The logs had been stolen from them—why wouldn't they want justice? It's very possible that the traffickers bribed government officials, or even that the officials themselves allowed the logs to be cut down.

Eventually, the traffickers were convicted only to have their conviction overturned a short time later. They were legally given the logs. But they couldn't move them! Singapore authorities told them they did not have the right paperwork to leave the country. China, where the traffickers wanted to ship the logs, said it would not accept them. The logs sit in the warehouse to this day, gradually being nibbled by termites, a rare treasure wasted and rotting.

Caper Corner

In 2024, authorities in the Dominican Republic arrested a man who was transporting **twenty-three planks of illegal ebony** in the back of his pickup truck. Ebony is a rare and precious wood that grows naturally in the Dominican Republic and is protected by law.

Caper Corner

Criminals don't just stick to trees. In 2021, authorities in Italy uncovered a cache of over a thousand **endangered cacti worth about $1.2 million**. Almost all the cacti had been stolen from the wilds of Chile, South America.

Scientists estimate the island of Madagascar split off from the continent of Africa about 160 million years ago. **Plants, animals, and ecosystems** evolved separately. About 92 to 95 percent of Madagascar's reptile and mammal life and 89 percent of its plants exist nowhere else on Earth.

Busy Port
The port at Singapore is one of the busiest in the world, with about 140,000 calling in every single year.

Heist Hero

Lawyer **Harotsilavo Rakotosan** normally handled corporate cases, not criminal cases. But when he heard about the rosewood heist, he thought he could help the government in Madagascar. The logs were cut down illegally. Then they were transported out of the country illegally. He thought he could easily make the case that they should be transported back to Madagascar. Harotsilavo didn't get the logs returned to Madagascar, but he did stand up for what was right: protecting rare and precious plants and trees.

Antwerp Diamond Heist

The garden at the back of the Antwerp World Diamond Center was dark and deserted when five shadowy figures stole in from a neighboring building. They were experienced Italian thieves, and they were there to break into one of the world's most secure vaults.

Deep under the Diamond Center, the vault held safe-deposit boxes filled with diamonds, gold, and gems from Antwerp's busy diamond district. The vault was protected by a three-ton steel door that was made to withstand twelve hours of drilling. A sensor would detect even the smallest vibration and set off alarms. The combination lock had one hundred million possible combinations. Inside the vault, heat and motion sensors would detect anyone's presence. Two metal plates also guarded the door, casting a magnetic shield across it, which set off an alarm when broken. In addition to the combination, a special foot-long key was needed to open the door.

This vault was thief-proof. But not to Leonardo Notarbartolo and his crew. They were expert lock-pickers, forgers, and electronics whizzes. They'd been planning this heist for more than two years. And tonight was the night.

Leonardo had already done advance work. He'd rented a safe-deposit box in the vault, and

Fast Facts

DATE: 2003

LOCATION: Antwerp, Belgium

LOOT: About $100 million in gold, cash, and jewels

on one of his visits, he'd stealthily installed a small camera to record the vault's combination. The video recording was streamed to a storage device that Leo had hidden inside a nearby fire extinguisher. Then, on the day of the heist, Leo visited his safe-deposit box inside the vault again. He'd sprayed ordinary hairspray around the vault. The oily aerosol would temporarily block the heat and motion sensor inside.

Once inside the building, the thieves covered the security cameras with black plastic. One of the thieves, called "The Genius," used sticky tape and a slab of metal to loosen the magnetic plates that guarded the door. He scooted them to the side while still maintaining the shield. No alarms were set off. The thieves unlocked the door with the key they found hanging in a utility room.

They were inside the vault.

Ring Leader Leonardo Notarbartolo masterminded the heist that took part in Antwerp's diamond district.

Time to work fast. They covered the motion and heat sensors with a Styrofoam shield. They used a hand-cranked drill to pry open each of the safe-deposit boxes, dumping gold bars, cash, and diamonds into duffel bags. As dawn broke over Antwerp, the thieves had to stop—their bags were getting too full.

Eventually, Leo and the team got out of the Diamond Center with $100 million. They split up the cash and loaded their trash from the heist into a car, then dumped it all on the road between Antwerp and Brussels. But that was a mistake.

When the owner of the land where the trash was dumped called the police to complain, the cops investigated. They found clues in the garbage that eventually led them to Leo and his gang. One clue was a salami sandwich. The half-eaten sandwich was found in the trash heap with a package for the salami nearby. When police searched Leo's apartment, they found a receipt for salami. They visited the store where Leo had purchased the meat, looked at the store's security video, and boom—there was one of Leo's gang, buying the salami.

During the search of Leo's apartment, the police also found diamonds in a personal safe and hidden in the shag of a rolled-up carpet that Leo's wife just happened to be taking out of the house. Eventually, Leo and his gang went to jail. By 2024, Leo was out of prison and back in Italy. Sorry? He's not sorry. "I would definitely do [the heist] again," he told a journalist. "But much better."

Caper Corner

Diamonds are other thieves' best friends, too. Following in Leo's footsteps, a gang of eight thieves nabbed **$50 million worth of diamonds** in Brussels, Belgium. There was no ultra-secure vault this time. Instead, the thieves broke through a fence at the **Brussels airport**, then broke into the cargo hold of a plane loaded with diamonds bound for Switzerland. Stealing away with the loot, the thieves went back out the hole in the fence. Later, they abandoned their getaway car and set fire to it to make it harder to trace.

No Rush
Once inside the vault, the thieves had all night to break open and empty the safe-deposit boxes.

Philadelphia Insectarium and Butterfly Pavilion Heist

The young woman raised the glass lid of the enclosure. Slipping a hand inside, she lifted out the giant, hairy tarantula. Carefully, she transferred the arachnid to a travel box she had waiting.

Others moved around the large exhibition room at the Philadelphia Insectarium and Butterfly Pavilion. One by one, they slipped cockroaches, geckoes, millipedes, and mantises into plastic carrying cases. Then, watched by the surveillance cameras, they tiptoed out, taking the live insects and reptiles with them.

Was this a heist?

When $40,000 worth of insects and reptiles disappeared from the Insectarium over the course of four days in August 2018, the answer seemed simple: It was a heist. After all, employees had been caught on camera taking the creatures out of the building. It seemed clear it was an inside job. The thieves probably meant to sell the creatures on the black market, the museum director John Cambridge guessed.

Fast Facts

DATE: 2018

LOCATION: Philadelphia, Pennsylvania

LOOT: About $40,000 worth of insects, reptiles, and arachnids

CASE OPEN!

Home for Bugs
The inside of an insectarium has conditions and plants to mimic the home habitats that the bugs come from.

Or did they? Three of the former employees were investigated by the FBI. They were considered suspects, but they were not arrested. The employees told the FBI that they didn't steal the insects. The Insectarium had been having money problems for a long time, they said. The exhibits were sitting empty, so the employees would bring in insects and reptiles from their own collections at home.

Eventually, the employees and director John Cambridge argued. The employees quit. When they left, they took their animals with them. There was no theft, they said. They were just taking back the animals they'd lent to the Insectarium.

The Insectarium no longer exists. John Cambridge stopped paying for the building, so the government came to take it. But when the sheriff arrived to take over the property, he found all the cages and aquariums smashed, the toilets demolished, and junk everywhere. Whoever had been working at the Insectarium on that last night had destroyed it as a kind prank on the sheriff. The insect heist remains unsolved, buried under the debris of a failed institution. Four years later, the case remains open.

The museum director accused the former employees of taking about seven thousand insects and other creatures from the Insectarium. Some were special stars, like the **desert hairy scorpion** and the **domino cockroach**. But others were insects being raised to feed the other critters.

Many of the people who worked at the Insectarium were interested in **entomology, the study of insects**. Entomology often examines the relationship between people and insects, both helpful and harmful. An entomologist might work with farmers to help them control pests in their crops. Or they might study the habitat of endangered insects to learn how best to protect them.

Rich Wildlife
The Philadelphia Insectarium was home to a wide range of wildlife, from geckos to brightly colored butterflies and even large spiders!

Solve It Yourself: Was the Insectarium Heist *Really* a Heist?

The employees all knew there were cameras in the Insectarium. Yet they didn't turn off the cameras, cover them, or try to hide from them. Instead, they calmly packed up the animals and **walked out in plain sight**, knowing they were being recorded. They even wore their employee uniforms and didn't cover their faces with hoods or masks. Would they be this obvious if they meant to sell the insects on the black market?

Police also discovered **employee uniforms** pinned to the wall in the Insectarium with a sharp butcher knife. Was this another sign that the employees were angry with their employer?

On the other hand, police only found some of the missing insects and reptiles at the employees' homes. Where did the others go? Were they sold on the black market, as the director John Cambridge alleged?

Theft of the *Mona Lisa*

Stealing the world's most famous work of art? In 1911, not a problem. But also in 1911? Not the world's most famous work of art.

In August 1911, the *Mona Lisa* wasn't a cultural icon. She was just a painting by Leonardo da Vinci, hanging in the Louvre Museum in Paris. Still, she was valuable. So, when an Italian handyman wanted to make a little money, he set his sights on the eyebrow-less lady with the mysterious smile.

Vincenzo Peruggia knew about the Louvre. He had been part of the crew that built the frame and glass case around the *Mona Lisa*. And Vincenzo knew that museum security was pretty light. It was easy for him and two accomplices to slip in before closing one night and hide in a supply closet.

As soon as it was morning, before the museum opened, they bustled out of the closet, yanked the Mona Lisa off the wall, and wrestled her out of her case and frame, which were abandoned in a hallway. With the painting covered with a blanket, the thieves climbed aboard an express train out of the city.

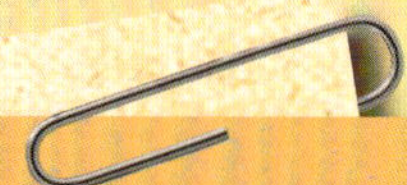

Fast Facts

DATE: 1911

LOCATION: Paris, France

LOOT: One priceless painting

Art Thief
Vincenzo Peruggia was able to hide in the museum overnight to steal the painting.

The countries of Europe were shifting their alliances with each other in 1911, and France and Germany were **starting to lose trust in each other**. By 1914, World War I began, with France, Great Britain, Russia, and others fighting against Germany and its allies.

Blank Space
Voncenzo left an empty space on the wall of the Louvre and kept hold of the painting for two years before it was discovered, as announced in this newspaper headline (right).

Once the museum realized the Mona Lisa had been stolen, the police sprang into action. Detectives began scouring the city for the painting, searching train cars, ships, and people at checkpoints. Various famous people were accused of stealing the painting. Did American tycoon J. P. Morgan orchestrate the theft so he could have the painting for his own collection? Did painter Pablo Picasso steal it? Or perhaps it was the German leader, Kaiser Wilhelm? After all, tensions between France and Germany were high.

Meanwhile, Vincenzo still had the painting. He'd hidden it in a trunk with a false bottom. He'd meant to sell it, but now too many people knew about the theft. He'd be sniffed out if he took the *Mona Lisa* to an art dealer. Instead, he left it in the trunk for over two years.

Finally, in December 1913, Vincenzo was ready to take a chance. He offered to sell it to an Italian art dealer, telling him that the painting could have a rightful home in Italy, rather than in France. But the art dealer wasn't buying Vincenzo's story. He called the police, who arrested Vincenzo.

Vincenzo was sentenced to eight months in prison. And the *Mona Lisa* was reframed and rehung on the walls of the Louvre, where she looks out to this day, still smiling.

A pushy amateur painter was the one who discovered that the Mona Lisa was missing. He was setting up to paint in the Louvre and saw the painting was gone. He insisted he could not paint **without the *Mona Lisa* present**. Museum officials thought the painting had been removed by museum photographers for a brief time. But when they investigated, they discovered the theft.

Heist Hero

The art dealer who turned Vincenzo in was named **Alfredo Geri**. He didn't take Vincenzo's offer to sell the painting, even though doing so would have returned the *Mona Lisa* to Italy. Instead, Geri talked to the head of the **Uffizi Gallery in Florence**, one of Italy's most important art museums. Geri and the museum head agreed that before they could do anything, they had to confirm that the painting was authentic. They told Vincenzo to bring his painting to Florence. There, a stamp on the back confirmed that it *was* the *Mona Lisa*. Geri told Vincenzo to wait, that they'd see about getting him a reward. But instead, Geri fetched the police and Vincenzo was nabbed.

Le Petit Parisien

5 centimes

Le plus fort tirage des journaux du monde entier

MALADIES SALUTAIRES

LA «JOCONDE» EST RETROUVÉE

Le célèbre tableau, proposé à un antiquaire, a été saisi à Florence et sera restitué à la France.

Menacé de destitution en cas d'erreur, M. Ricci, directeur des Beaux-Arts d'Italie, garantit énergiquement l'authenticité de l'œuvre confisquée.

La Fin d'une Conquête

LA « JOCONDE »

LA RUSSIE DEMANDE aux puissances de rappeler leurs troupes de Chine

Vincenzo fought in the Italian army during World War I and died in 1925.

Itaú Unibanco Heist

This was going to be an easy job. Put on gray coveralls. Gather a saw, a blowtorch, a set of drills. Then stroll into the Itaú Unibanco bank in São Paulo, Brazil, and announce that you're there to fix the alarm system.

Fast Facts

DATE: 2011

LOCATION: São Paulo, Brazil

LOOT: $59 million in gems, gold, and cash

CASE OPEN!

No matter that it's midnight on a Saturday. No matter that there are ten of you. The guard? He's not going to check you out or hit a panic button. Instead, he's going to wave you through.

That was the experience for a group of thieves who robbed the Itaú Unibanco the night of August 27, 2011. After their jaunt past the security guards, the gang took their time breaking into 170 safe-deposit boxes and emptying them of cash, rubies, emeralds, and gold. The thieves loaded their bags with about $59 million worth of precious metals, gems, and cash.

Big Bank
Itaú Unibano is the largest bank in Brazil and Latin America, and employs nearly 100,000 people.

But where were the police? Nowhere. No alarms went off during the ten hours the gang spent emptying the vault. The gang did take guns from two security guards, but no one tried to escape. In fact, the criminals even ordered fast food, ate it, and left the wrappers lying around while they worked.

Even more strangely, the São Paulo police didn't even start their investigation until a week after the robbery. They didn't get around to interviewing the two security guards until four days after that. Was this an inside job? Were the security guards in on the heist? Were the police in on the crime as well?

"No," the police head said when he was asked. The police weren't involved in the crime. And investigators were able to identify the robbers. The gang had destroyed most of the security cameras during the heist, but a few had survived. From that tape, investigators confirmed the identities of twelve robbers. And yet, only one was arrested. And the loot? Some of the owners of the safe-deposit boxes hired private firms to track down their precious jewels. Some were found. Some never were. And the case remains, to this day, open.

Caper Corner

Some of the Itaú Unibanco thieves may have been involved in another high-profile caper, also in Brazil. In 2005, in the northern Brazilian city of Fortaleza, a gang dug a tunnel from a nearby house into the **Banco Central (Central Bank)**. The tunnel took them three months to dig. When they finally broke through into the bank, they made off with the equivalent of $95 million, the biggest bank robbery in Brazil's history.

Taking Their Time
The thieves took the whole night to open and empty safe-deposit boxes in the bank's vault.

One safe-deposit box owner lost not only a **diamond necklace** in the heist but also a ring with a diamond as big as a cherry. Another lost fifty-eight emeralds.

Brazil is giant. It is the fifth largest country in the world and covers half the land in South America. It also has the **fifth largest population on Earth**. Every year, Brazil hosts the world's biggest party, Rio Carnival, when two million people take to the streets to dance and celebrate in the days leading up to Lent.

Caper Corner

The burglars said they were **alarm repairmen**, but they had an even more solid cover for their story: The bank was under renovations, and the guards had been told that people might be coming in to work at night.

300-Million-Yen Robbery

"Stop! Stop!" the police officer on the motorcycle yelled. He screeched up beside a bank van laden with cash. The four bank guards in the van stared out. "There's a bomb under that car!" the officer on the motorcycle yelled. "Get out! Get out!"

The guards leapt from the van as the officer crawled underneath. Smoke began to curl out. It seemed that the officer had gotten there just in time.

It was December 10, 1968. The van was driving about ¥300 million (about $7,440,000 today) from the Nihon Shintaku Ginko Bank to the Toshiba factory in the suburbs of Tokyo, Japan. The money was meant for holiday bonuses for the factory workers. And the idea of a bomb in the van wasn't totally new. One of the bank's managers had gotten a bomb threat just days before.

Fast Facts

DATE: December 10, 1968

LOCATION: Tokyo, Japan

LOOT: About ¥300 million (about $7,440,000 today)

CASE OPEN!

Motorcycle Madness
This photo shows the motocycle used by the thief to stop the security van.

"Your manager's house has been bombed," the officer panted from under the car. "This van's been wired with dynamite." Flames and smoke licked out from under the van as the guards huddled together, staring.

Then, the officer climbed into the driver's seat and drove the bank van away.

It had all been a setup. There was no bomb threat. There was no dynamite. The smoke and flames? Just a flare the "officer" set off as he crawled under the van.

The criminal was gone, and the real police got to work. One hundred and seventy thousand police officers eventually worked on the case. They investigated 110,000 suspects, but after seven years, the investigation ended without an arrest. After twenty years, Japanese law says that the suspect, whoever he was, was cleared and could speak out without fear of arrest. But no one came forward. And no one has since. The money has never been found. No suspects have been arrested. And almost sixty years later, the case remains unsolved.

Caper Corner

In a later Tokyo robbery, the criminals didn't get away so easily. In 2023, robbers pulled up on a motorbike in front of a store selling gold and silver. Leaping off their bike, they pushed their way into the store and began smashing the cases containing the precious metals. But then, they got a shock. One of the store employees came out swinging a **sasumata, a type of ancient weapon**. This long pole with a spear-like fork on the end was used by samurai security forces to pin down criminals. The employee smashed the criminals' motorbike with the sasumata, and the criminals fled empty-handed.

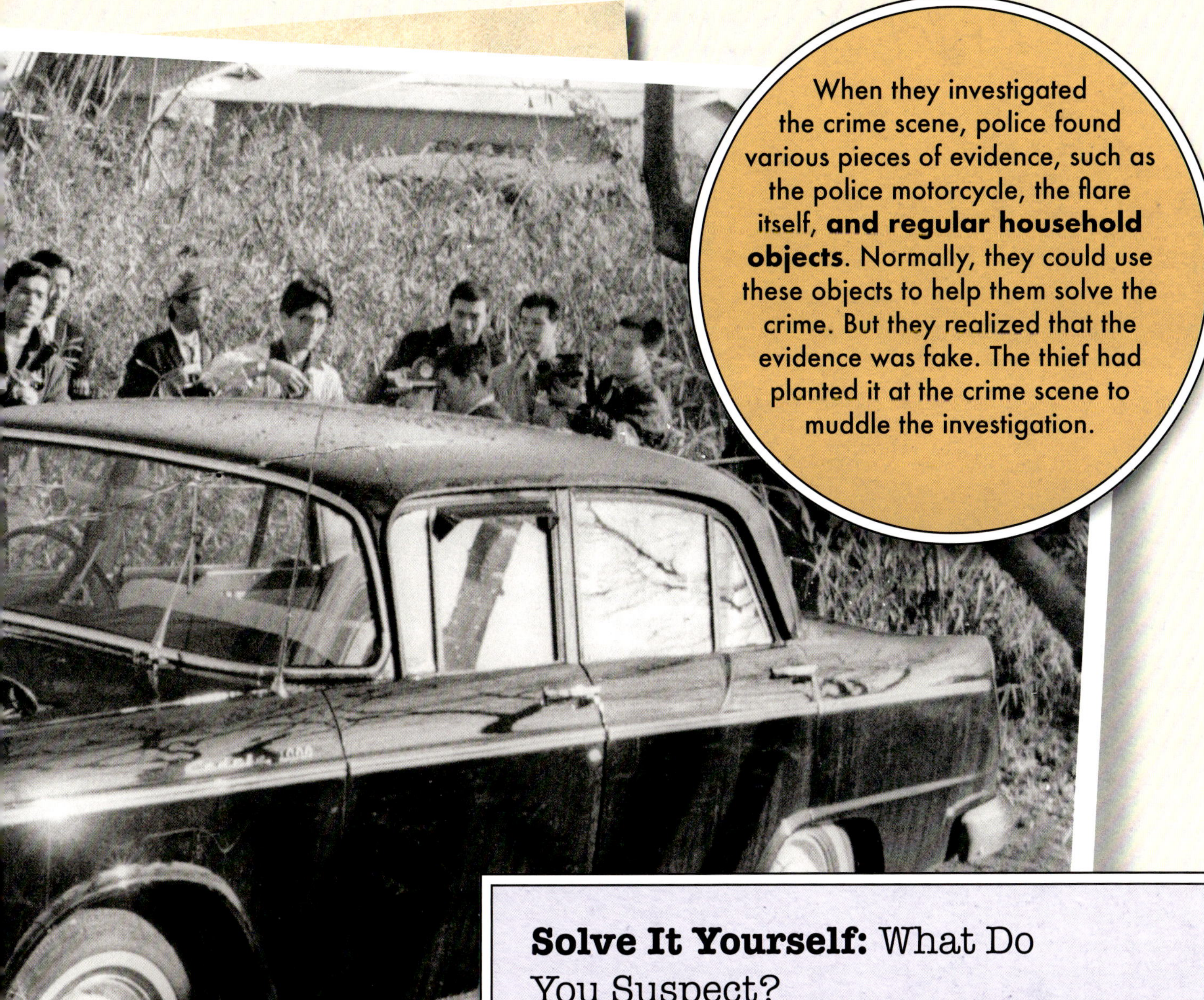

When they investigated the crime scene, police found various pieces of evidence, such as the police motorcycle, the flare itself, **and regular household objects**. Normally, they could use these objects to help them solve the crime. But they realized that the evidence was fake. The thief had planted it at the crime scene to muddle the investigation.

Solve It Yourself: What Do You Suspect?

This 300-million-yen robbery has never been solved. At first, police thought the culprit might be the nineteen-year-old **son of an officer**. He was the leader of a youth gang. Then, the police thought it might be a driver working at a **Canadian government office** in Tokyo. He looked like a composite photo the police were using. But he had an alibi, too. He was taking a test with people watching him at the time of the heist.

Seven years after the heist, a friend of the nineteen-year-old was found with large amounts of cash. But even though the police questioned him, they couldn't prove the money came from the bank robbery.

Photofit
Police recovered this car, which they believed was used by the thief after he emptied the van. They also released an artist's impression of what the theif looked like (left).

Where in the World

1. São Paulo, Brazil
(Itaú Unibanco Heist)

2. Paris, France
(*Mona Lisa* Theft)

3. Tokyo, Japan
(300-Million-Yen Robbery)

4. Philadelphia, Pennsylvania
(Philadelphia Insectarium and Butterfly Pavilion Heist)

5. Boston, Massachusetts
(Isabella Stewart Gardner Museum Heist)

6. London, England
(Hatton Garden Heist)

7. Eugowra, Australia
(Eugowra Gold Robbery)

10
10
6
12
2
3
11
11
7
8. Québec, Canada
(Maple Syrup Heist)
9. Bermuda
(Tucker Cross Theft)
10. Coast of England/Gdańsk, Poland
(The Last Judgment Heist)
11. Madagascar/Jurong, Singapore
(Madagascar Rosewood Heist)
12. Antwerp, Belgium
(Antwerp Diamond Heist)

Timeline

1455–
In Germany, Gutenberg Bible is the first book ever published

1473–
The Last Judgment Heist

1492–
Christopher Columbus first lands in the Caribbean.

1776–
The Declaration of Independence is signed.

1861–
The American Civil War begins in South Carolina.

1862–
Eugowra Gold Robbery

1889–
The Eiffel Tower is completed in Paris.

1455 1473 1492 1776 1861 1862 1889

1990 2001 2003 2010 2011 2013

1990–
Isabella Stewart Gardner Museum Heist

2001–
Planes hit the World Trade Center and the Pentagon in the September 11 terrorist attacks.

2003–
Antwerp Diamond Heist

2010–
Taylor Swift wins her first GRAMMY award.

2011–
Maple Syrup Heist, Itaú Unibanco Heist

2013–
The Black Lives Matter social justice movement begins.

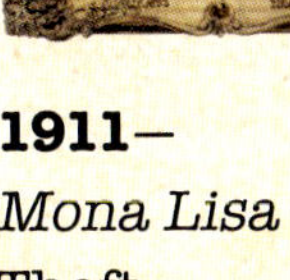

1901— Australia becomes a nation.

1911— *Mona Lisa* Theft

1929— The American stock market crashes on Wall Street, setting off the Great Depression.

1939— World War II begins when Nazi Germany invades Poland.

1968— 300-Million-Yen Robbery

1969— The Woodstock Music Festival is held in Bethel, New York.

1975— Tucker Cross Heist

1901 | 1911 | 1929 | 1939 | 1968 | 1969 | 1975

2014 | 2015 | 2018 | 2020 | 2022 | 2025

2014— Madagascar Rosewood Heist

2015— Hatton Garden Heist

2018— Philadelphia Insectarium and Butterfly Pavilion Heist

2020— The World Health Organization declares COVID-19 a pandemic.

2022— Queen Elizabeth II dies.

2025— Donald Trump is sworn in as President of the United States for the second time.

Glossary

alibi: proof that someone was not in the place that a crime was committed

altar: a raised area in a church or another place of worship, used in religious ceremonies

black market: illegal trade in goods in violation of the law

blowtorch: a tool that has a very hot gasoline flame increased by a burst of air

commissioned: ordered to be made in exchange for payment

dynamite: a type of explosive material

executed: accomplished

geckoes: small, nocturnal lizards, often with sticky toe pads

heist: a crime in which valuable things are stolen or taken

hydraulic: operated by the pressure of water

icon: a person or thing that is admired for having influence or significance

karat: a unit for measuring how much gold is in a piece of jewelry or metal

mafia: a secret criminal society

Mughal: a Muslim dynasty that ruled in northern India from about 1500 to 1700

sheriff: the law enforcement officer of a county

termites: pale-colored insects that live in colonies and eat wood

trafficking: the act of buying or selling goods illegally

triptych: a picture or carving in three panels set side-by-side

Further Reading

Books

Jewel Heists (High-Stakes Heists)
by Kenny Abdo

The Mona Lisa Vanishes: A Legendary Painter, a Shocking Heist, and the Birth of a Global Celebrity
by Nicholas Day

Heists (The Hidden World of Crime)
by C. M. Johnson and John Willis

Curious Cases: True Crime for Kids: Hijinks, Heists, Mysteries, and More
by Rebecca Valley

Famous Robberies
by Soledad Romero

The Story of Paintings: A History of Art for Children
by Mick Manning

Gems for Kids
by Lee Hall and Ashley Hall

Websites

Art History Kids: https://www.arthistorykids.com/

National Geographic Kids: Incredible Insects: https://kids.nationalgeographic.com/videos/topic/incredible-insects

Maple from Canada: https://kids.maplefromcanada.ca/

Podcasts

Heist Podcast: https://podcasts.apple.com/us/podcast/heist-podcast/id1329231773

The Mystery Kids Podcast: The Great Diamond Heist: https://podcasts.apple.com/il/podcast/124-the-great-diamond-heist/id1522936362?i=1000689480302

Curious Kid Podcast: https://www.curiouskidpodcast.com/

References

ABC News. "How a Bushranger Gang Pulled Off Australia's Biggest Gold Heist." August 26, 2018. https://www.abc.net.au/news/2018-08-26/how-a-bushranger-gang-pulled-off-australias-biggest-gold-heist/10152580.

Araluen Valley History. "The Failed Araluen Gold Escort Robbery." https://araluenvalley-history.com.au/bushrangers/the-failed-araluen-gold-escort-robbery/.

Art Publika Mag. "Six of History's Most Incredible Art Heists." July 1, 2018. https://www.artpublikamag.com/post/2018/07/01/six-of-historys-most-incredible-art-heists.

ARTnews. "The Greatest Art Heists of All Time." March 25, 2023. https://www.artnews.com/list/art-news/artists/greatest-art-heists-of-all-time-1234583441/.

BBC News. "Hatton Garden Robbery: Thieves Sentenced to Prison." December 21, 2015. https://www.bbc.com/news/uk-england-london-35231864.

BBC News. "Maple Syrup Heist: Canada's 'Liquid Gold' Stolen." December 22, 2015. https://www.bbc.com/news/business-35028380.

BBC News. "Rare Diamond Stolen in $50 Million Heist." February 17, 2013. https://www.bbc.com/news/world-europe-21504112.

Bernews. "Teddy Tucker Cross Replica Unveiled." December 2024. https://bernews.com/2024/12/teddy-tucker-cross-replica-unveiled/.

Cosmopolitan. "Hatton Garden Heist: The Inside Story." https://www.cosmopolitan.com/uk/reports/a60809952/hatton-garden-heist/.

Daily Art Magazine. "The Biggest Art Heists in History." https://www.dailyartmagazine.com/biggest-art-heists-in-history/.

DAME Magazine. "Maple Syrup Monopolies Are a Sticky Business." August 3, 2022. https://www.damemagazine.com/2022/08/03/maple-syrup-monopolies-are-a-sticky-business/.

Forbes. "The True Story Behind Prime Video's 'The Sticky': The Great Canadian Maple Syrup Heist." December 6, 2024. https://www.forbes.com/sites/monicamercuri/2024/12/06/the-true-story-behind-prime-video-the-sticky-the-great-canadian-maple-syrup-heist/.

Ground News. "Visiting Italy with Leonardo Notarbartolo, the Brain Behind Antwerp's Biggest Diamond Heist: 'I Would Definitely Do It Again, but Much Better.'" February 8, 2021. https://ground.news/article/visiting-italy-with-leonardo-notarbartolo-the-brain-behind-antwerps-biggest-diamond-heist-i-would-definitely-do-it-again-but-much-better.

History Channel. "The Heist That Made the Mona Lisa Famous." History.com, August 21, 2018. https://www.history.com/news/the-heist-that-made-the-mona-lisa-famous.

Irish Examiner. "The Story Behind the Irish Art Heist." July 21, 2019. https://www.irishexaminer.com/world/arid-20216592.html.

Isabella Stewart Gardner Museum. "Isabella Stewart Gardner Museum's Board of Trustees Extends $10 Million Reward for Return of 13 Works Stolen in 1990." https://www.gardnermuseum.org/isabella-stewart-gardner-museums-board-trustees-extends-10-million-reward-return-13-works-stolen.

Isabella Stewart Gardner Museum. "Theft Story." https://www.gardnermuseum.org/about/theft-story.

Isabella Stewart Gardner Museum. "Theft." https://www.gardnermuseum.org/organization/theft.

Japan Today. "Shop Employee Fights Off Three Robbers with Polearm in Ueno." March 5, 2023. https://japantoday.com/category/crime/shop-employee-fights-off-three-robbers-with-polearm.

JSTOR. "The Art of the Heist: Theft and Recovery of Art." https://www.jstor.org/stable/3045833?seq=1#page_scan_tab_contents.

Lawyer Monthly. "Cracking the Gardner Heist: Eight Clues to Unlocking the World's Greatest Art Mystery." November 2024. https://www.lawyer-monthly.com/2024/11/cracking-the-gardner-heist-eight-clues-to-unlocking-the-worlds-greatest-art-mystery/.

Library of Congress. "Theft of the Mona Lisa." Chronicling America, last modified March 14, 2023. https://guides.loc.gov/chronicling-america-theft-mona-lisa.

Lismore City News. "Biggest Gold Heist in Australian History: 160 Years On from Escort Rock." September 1, 2021. https://www.lismorecitynews.com.au/story/7833288/biggest-gold-heist-in-australian-history-160-years-on-from-escort-rock/.

Mental Floss. "The Tucker's Cross Treasure Mystery." January 6, 2022. https://www.mentalfloss.com/posts/tuckers-cross-treasure-mystery.

MoneyWeek. "10 December 1968: The 300 Million Yen Robbery." December 10, 2018. https://moneyweek.com/363610/10-december-1968-the-300-million-yen-robbery.

Muzeum Narodowe Gdańsk. "The Last Judgement." https://web.archive.org/web/20070701003920/http:/www.muzeum.narodowe.gda.pl/last_judgement.htm.

NBC Philadelphia. "FBI Involved in Hunt for Rare Insects Stolen from Philadelphia Museum." February 23, 2018. https://www.nbcphiladelphia.com/news/local/fbi-involved-in-hunt-for-rare-insects-stolen-from-philadelphia-museum/214294/.

Northeast Times. "What Really Happened to Those Stolen Insectarium Bugs?" February 25, 2022. https://northeasttimes.com/2022/02/25/what-really-happened-to-those-stolen-insectarium-bugs/.

NPR. "The Theft That Made the Mona Lisa a Masterpiece." July 30, 2011. https://www.npr.org/2011/07/30/138800110/the-theft-that-made-the-mona-lisa-a-masterpiece.

Radio Times. "What Is the Real-Life Story Behind ITV's Heist Drama Hatton Garden?" https://www.radiotimes.com/tv/drama/what-is-the-real-life-story-behind-itvs-heist-drama-hatton-garden/.

Scope Project. "The $300,000,000 Bank Heist." Scope Project, Issue 7, October 2021. https://www.scopeproject.org/300000000-bank-heist-issue-7.

South China Morning Post. "Who Was the Mysterious Motorcyclist Behind the Infamous Japanese Heist?" April 3, 2019. https://www.scmp.com/news/asia/east-asia/article/2177413/who-was-mysterious-motorcyclist-behind-infamous-japanese-heist.

Teddy Tucker. "Tucker Cross: The Mysterious Treasure of Bermuda." September 25, 2017. https://www.teddytucker.com/articles/2017/9/25/tucker-cross.

The Bermudian. "Legacy of a Legendary Explorer." Accessed March 18, 2024. https://www.thebermudian.com/people/legacy-of-a-legendary-explorer/.

The Canadian Encyclopedia. "Great Canadian Maple Syrup Heist." Accessed March 18, 2024. https://www.thecanadianencyclopedia.ca/en/article/great-canadian-maple-syrup-heist.

The Guardian. "Basil, the Hatton Garden Robbery's Michael Seed, Was the Best Alarm Specialist in London." March 16, 2019. https://www.theguardian.com/uk-news/2019/mar/16/basil-hatton-garden-robbery-michael-seed-best-alarm-specialist-in-london.

The Guardian. "Explorers Unlock the Mystery of Pirate King Henry Avery, Who Vanished After Huge Heist at Sea." March 30, 2024. https://www.theguardian.com/world/2024/mar/30/explorers-unlock-the-mystery-of-pirate-king-henry-avery-who-vanished-after-huge-heist-at-sea.

The Guardian. "Hatton Garden Jewel Heist: Cops, Robbers, Clients." April 10, 2015. https://www.theguardian.com/uk-news/2015/apr/10/hatton-garden-jewel-heist-cops-robbers-clients.

The Guardian. "Maple Syrup Heist: The Theft of Quebec's Liquid Gold." December 22, 2014. https://www.theguardian.com/business/2014/dec/22/maple-syrup-heist-quebec-canada.

The Guardian. "Maple Syrup Heist: Thief Ordered to Repay Stolen Goods." April 1, 2022. https://www.theguardian.com/world/2022/apr/01/maple-syrup-heist-theif-ordered-repay-stolen-goods-canada.

The Guardian. "One Last Job: Inside Story of the Hatton Garden Heist." Last modified January 23, 2016. https://www.theguardian.com/uk-news/2016/jan/23/one-last-job-inside-story-of-the-hatton-garden-heist.

The New York Times. "Around the World: For London's Easter, a $7 Million Robbery." April 6, 1983. https://www.nytimes.com/1983/04/06/world/around-the-world-for-london-s-easter-a-7-million-robbery.html?module=inline.

The New York Times. "Stolen Bugs: The Insect Heist That Shook Philadelphia." August 30, 2018. https://www.nytimes.com/2018/08/30/us/stolen-bugs-insects-philadelphia.html.

The New York Times. "Unsolved Gardner Museum Heist." Last modified March 18, 2024. https://www.nytimes.com/2024/03/18/arts/design/unsolved-gardner-museum-heist.html.

The Royal Gazette. "Unravelling the Mystery of the Tucker Cross." January 11, 2016. https://www.royalgazette.com/arts-entertainment/lifestyle/article/20160111/unravelling-the-mystery-of-the-tucker-cross/.

The True Crime Database. "Antwerp Diamond Heist." https://www.thetruecrimedatabase.com/case_file/antwerp-diamond-heist/.

The Week. "How the Real Hatton Garden Robbery Played Out." https://theweek.com/63246/how-the-real-hatton-garden-robbery-played-out.

Time. "The Maple Syrup Heist: The Sticky Truth Behind Amazon's New Documentary." March 19, 2022. https://time.com/7200222/maple-syrup-heist-the-sticky-amazon/.

WBUR. "LastSeen: The Gardner Heist & Missing Art." Last modified August 20, 2018. https://www.wbur.org/news/2018/08/20/lastseen-gardner-heist-missing-art.

Web Gallery of Art. "The Last Judgment." https://www.wga.hu/html_m/m/memling/1early3/02last.html.

WGBH. "34 Years After Gardner Heist, the Museum's Director of Security Is Still on the Case." Last modified March 18, 2024. https://www.wgbh.org/news/local/2024-03-18/34-years-after-gardner-heist-the-museums-director-of-security-is-still-on-the-case.

WHYY. "Documentary Promises Inside Look at 2018 Heist at Philly's Insectarium." July 20, 2020. https://whyy.org/articles/documentary-promises-inside-look-at-2018-heist-at-phillys-insectarium/.

WHYY. "Financial Strife at Philadelphia Insectarium Museum." September 14, 2018. https://whyy.org/articles/financial-strife-philadelphia-insectarium-museum/.

WHYY. "Financial Strife at Philadelphia Insectarium Museum." September 14, 2018. https://whyy.org/articles/financial-strife-philadelphia-insectarium-museum/.

WHYY. "Philadelphia Insectarium Evicted Due to Building Damage." December 3, 2020. https://whyy.org/articles/philadelphia-insectarium-evicted-building-damage/.

Wired. "The Diamond Heist That Shocked the World." March 13, 2009. https://www.wired.com/2009/03/ff-diamonds-2/.